Grammaropolis PRESENTS

Izzy the Interjection

Written by Coert Voorhees

Illustrations by Powerhouse Animation

Meet the Parts of Speech

I name a specific person, place, thing, or idea. It's a big responsibility, naming things—a responsibility that requires a certain attention to detail.

Nelson the Noun

Some people say I'm all over the place. Some people call me a ball of energy. I take that as a compliment, because I just like to go, go, go!

Vinny the Action Verb

I take the place of one or more Nouns or Pronouns. I always want the Noun's job, and I hang out with the Verb and Adjective.

Roger the Pronoun

I'm perfectly happy to link Nouns and Pronouns with the appropriate Adjectives, but it's not like I'm going to expend a lot of energy doing so.

Lucy the Linking Verb

I modify a Noun or Pronoun. I tell what kind, which one, how many, or how much. I pride myself on being the most artistic of the parts of speech.

Jake the Adjective

Gather 'round everybody and let's have ourselves a wonderful time. I just love bringing words and groups of words together, don't you?

Connie the Conjunction

I modify a Verb, Adjective, or other Adverb. I tell how, when, where, to what extent, and under what condition. I often end in –ly, but I don't have to.

Benny the Adverb

I express emotion!! Yep, I'm always here, always ready with my commas and exclamation points, just in case.

Izzy the Interjection

They call me Preposition because I'm pre-positioned. I'm first. At the front. Before every other word in the phrase? Got it?

Li'l Pete the Preposition

I am a chameleon. A spy. An undercover operative. I infiltrate the sentence and act as whatever part of speech suits me.

Slang

IZZY THE INTERJECTION

© 2019 Grammaropolis

Graphic Design by Mckee Frazior
Printed by Friesens, Altona, Manitoba, Canada

Text and Illustrations © 2011 by Grammaropolis LLC

This book is typeset in Komika Text

Distributed throughout the world
by Ingram Publisher Services
www.ingrambook.com

Printed in Canada

She expressed strong emotion with an exclamation mark.

Wow! These Crunchy Flakes sure are crunchy! Yeah!

She spent some time with Jake and his new a puppy.

She helped out when Li'l Pete finally understood advanced propulsion techniques.

But because she wasn't grammatically related to the rest of the sentence, she was often lonely when there was no emotion to express.

Hello?
Um, where is everyone?

14

So she sat down and waited for something to happen.

Until finally something *did* happen.
MOVE IT
Moving Company
Uh oh!

Izzy leapt to her feet and used a comma to express mild emotion.

Hey, Roger. Yo, wake up.

She hopped into the car, shoved Roger to the side, and slammed on the brakes.

Aaaahhh!

After that, there were plenty of interjections to go around.

Stop!
Do not read.

_____

_____

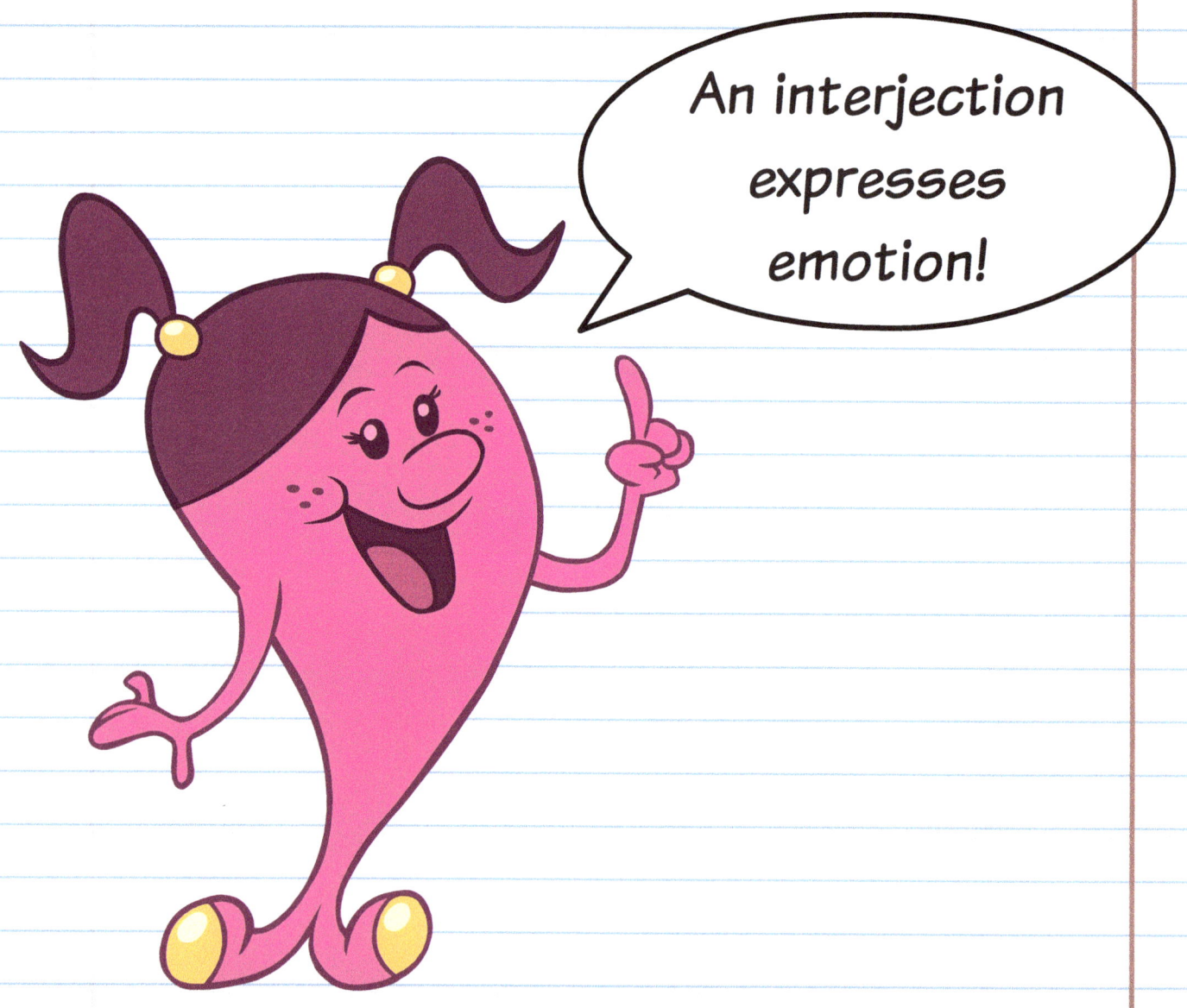

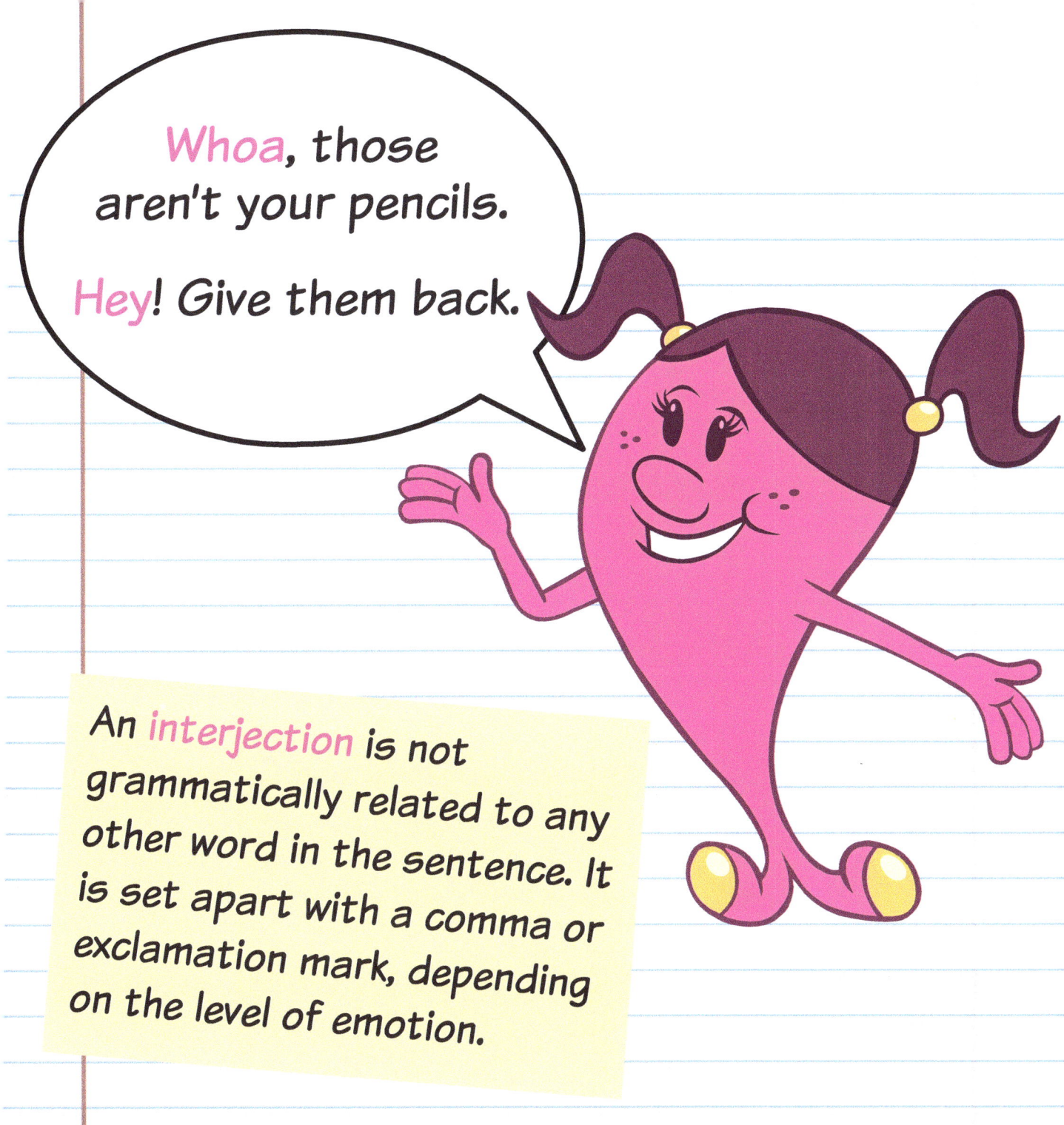

MILD EMOTION

Mild emotion is set apart by a comma.

Wow, those potato chips sure were expensive.

Hey, stop looking at me like that.

Gee, your friends are nice.

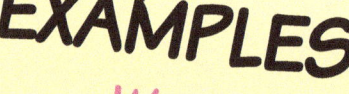

EXAMPLES
Wow

Hey

Gee

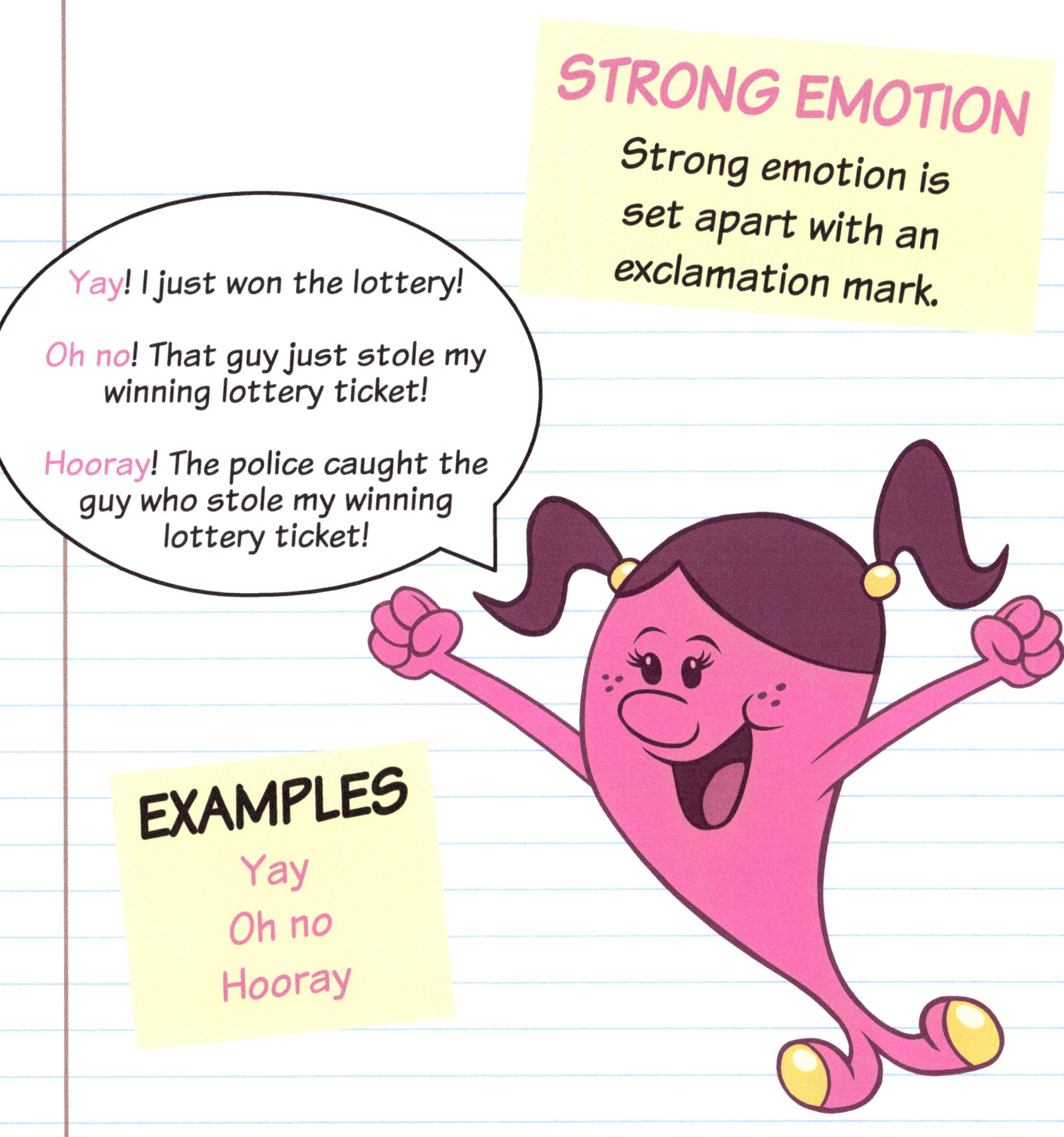

www.ingramcontent.com/pod-product-compliance
Lightning Source LLC
LaVergne TN
LVHW071213200326
834410LV00018B/576